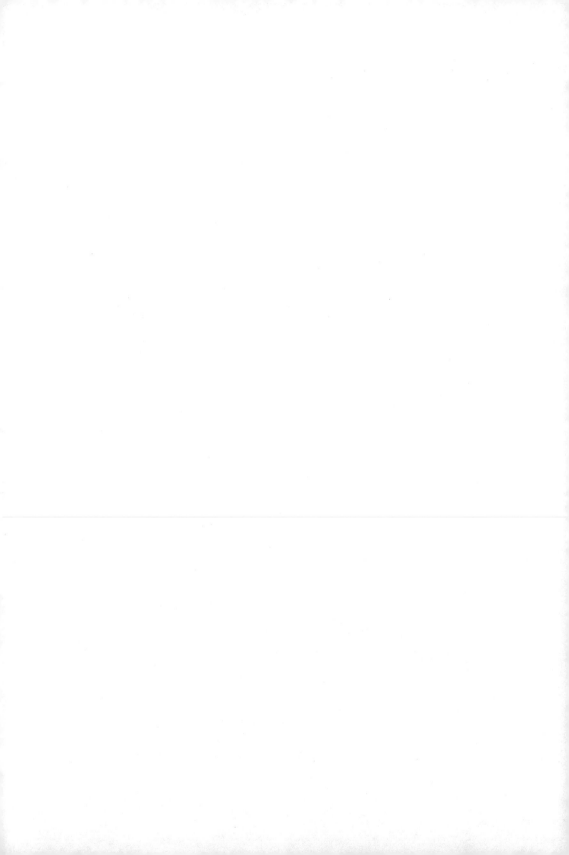

Sibling Rivalry

Relational Problems Involving
Brothers and Sisters

THE ENCYCLOPEDIA OF PSYCHOLOGICAL DISORDERS

Senior Consulting Editor Carol C. Nadelson, M.D.
Consulting Editor Claire E. Reinburg

Sibling Rivalry
Relational Problems Involving Brothers and Sisters

Elizabeth Russell Connelly

CHELSEA HOUSE PUBLISHERS
Philadelphia

The ENCYCLOPEDIA OF PSYCHOLOGICAL DISORDERS *provides up-to-date information on the history of, causes and effects of, and treatment and therapies for problems affecting the human mind. The titles in this series are not intended to take the place of the professional advice of a psychiatrist or mental health care professional.*

Chelsea House Publishers
Editor in Chief: Stephen Reginald
Managing Editor: James D. Gallagher
Production Manager: Pamela Loos
Art Director: Sara Davis
Director of Photography: Judy L. Hasday
Senior Production Editor: Lisa Chippendale

Staff for SIBLING RIVALRY
Prepared by P. M. Gordon Associates, Philadelphia
Picture Researcher: Gillian Speeth, Picture This
Associate Art Director: Takeshi Takahashi
Cover Designer: Brian Wible

The Chelsea House World Wide Web site address is
http://www.chelseahouse.com

First Printing

9 8 7 6 5 4 3 2 1

Library of Congress Cataloging-in-Publication Data

Connelly, Elizabeth Russell.

Sibling rivalry: relational problems involving brothers and sisters / by Elizabeth Russell Connelly.
    p. cm. — (Encyclopedia of psychological disorders)
Includes bibliographical references and index.
ISBN 0-7910-4952-3
1. Sibling abuse—Juvenile literature. 2. Sibling rivalry—Juvenile literature.
3. Brothers and sisters—Mental health—Juvenile literature. [1. Sibling abuse.
2. Brothers and sisters.] I. Title. II. Series: Connelly, Elizabeth Russell.
Encyclopedia of psychological disorders.
RJ507.S53C66 1999
618.92'85822—dc21   98-56102
                                                                          CIP
                                                                           AC

CONTENTS

PSYCHOLOGICAL DISORDERS AND THEIR EFFECT

CAROL C. NADELSON, M.D.
PRESIDENT AND CHIEF EXECUTIVE OFFICER,
The American Psychiatric Press

There are a wide range of problems that are considered psychological disorders, including mental and emotional disorders, problems related to alcohol and drug abuse, and some diseases that cause both emotional and physical symptoms. Psychological disorders often begin in early childhood, but during adolescence we see a sharp increase in the number of people affected by these disorders. It has been estimated that about 20 percent of the U.S. population will have some form of mental disorder sometime during their lifetime. Some psychological disorders appear following severe stress or trauma. Others appear to occur more often in some families and may have a genetic or inherited component. Still other disorders do not seem to be connected to any cause we can yet identify. There has been a great deal of attention paid to learning about the causes and treatments of these disorders, and exciting new research has taught us a great deal in the last few decades.

The fact that many new and successful treatments are available makes it especially important that we reject old prejudices and outmoded ideas that consider mental disorders to be untreatable. If psychological problems are identified early, it is possible to prevent serious consequences. We should not keep these problems hidden or feel shame that we or a member of our family has a mental disorder. Some people believe that something they said or did caused a mental disorder. Some people think that these disorders are "only in your head" so that you could "snap out of it" if you made the effort. This type of thinking implies that a treatment is a matter of willpower or motivation. It is a terrible burden for someone who is suffering to be blamed for their misery, and often people with psychological disorders are not treated compassionately. We hope that the information in this book will teach you about various mental illnesses.

The problems covered in the volumes in the ENCYCLOPEDIA OF PSYCHOLOGICAL DISORDERS were selected because they are of particular importance to young adults, because they affect them directly or because they affect family and friends. There are individual volumes on reading disorders, attention deficit and disruptive behavior disorders, and dementia—all of these are related to our abilities to learn and integrate information from the world around us. There are books on drug abuse that provide useful information about the effects of these drugs and treatments that are available for those individuals who have drug problems. Some of the books concentrate on one of the most common mental disorders, depression. Others deal with eating disorders, which are dangerous illnesses that affect a large number of young adults, especially women.

Most of the public attention paid to these disorders arises from a particular incident involving a celebrity that awakens us to our own vulnerability to psychological problems. These incidents of celebrities or public figures revealing their own psychological problems can also enable us to think about what we can do to prevent and treat these types of problems.

Even the best sibling relationships have some difficulties. But only when the problems become severe are they classified as psychological disorders.

OVERVIEW: PROBLEMS IN SIBLING RELATIONS

For some people, the term *sibling rivalry* may conjure up the picture of an older brother provoking them until they cry or of a younger sister exclaiming, "I'm telling Mom!" Anyone who has a sibling most likely has a closet full of stories about teasing brothers and bossy sisters, or vice versa. Although such experiences are typical of many sibling relationships, they are not considered severe or traumatic in the long term. No matter how distressing they may seem at the time, they don't usually push brothers and sisters to the point of needing professional counseling.

However, there are exceptional circumstances in which brothers and sisters may suffer more than the average. These may include being the victim of severe sibling aggression, growing up with a sibling who has a mental or physical disability, grappling with and overcoming the effects of sibling incest, or dealing with the death of a sibling. This volume in the ENCYCLOPEDIA OF PSYCHOLOGICAL DISORDERS attempts to illuminate the more severe difficulties that arise between brothers and sisters who are confronted with such traumatic experiences.

Chapter 1 introduces the reader to the topic, outlining the separate categories and contrasting healthy and normal conflict between brothers and sisters with behavior that should raise a red flag. Chapter 2 traces the history of these problems—the ways they have been defined and regarded through the ages. The following chapters then explore each of the categories in more detail, describing the likely causes and the behavior and feelings typical of each kind of problem. These chapters also highlight the various treatment options and resources that can help a child or teen overcome the emotional and psychological strain of sibling relational difficulties.

Because children learn a great deal from their brothers and sisters, sibling relationships have a profound influence on psychological development.

1

WHAT ARE SIBLING RELATIONAL PROBLEMS?

S ome of us may feel that simply having a sibling is a problem. Then there are those who wonder what they would do without their beloved brother or sister—their confidant and the bedrock of their support system. During the teenage years, we tend to relate more to our friends than to our family, but the sibling bond remains important. More than 80 percent of American children have at least one sister or brother, and the relationships between siblings help shape the mutual development of a wide variety of skills.

From our brothers and sisters, we learn how to communicate with others, behave socially, handle stress, negotiate for things we desire, express our feelings, and develop our thinking. The relationship between siblings influences each child's self-image, moral development, and choice of activities, among other things. The learning process starts at an early age, and the lessons stay with us throughout our lives. Often, too, these lessons differ substantially from the ones we learn from our parents.

Parent-child conversations tend to focus on caregiving and control. As children develop, their parents generally represent authority and power. Siblings, in contrast, provide a child's first introduction to social parameters—how to fit in as well as how to stand up for oneself. Especially if children are close in age and if they interact as equals, their interaction can help them develop perspective about their place in the world, moral maturity, and competence in relating to other youngsters.

This is the type of influence that sibling relationships usually have, but how do brothers and sisters affect one another under extraordinary circumstances? *Sibling rivalry* is a fairly common term, one that parents may use to dismiss quarreling and other conflicts between their children. Whether siblings have a relationship that is normally warm and stable or tumultuous, rivalry will occur throughout their early lives, and often into adulthood. However, there

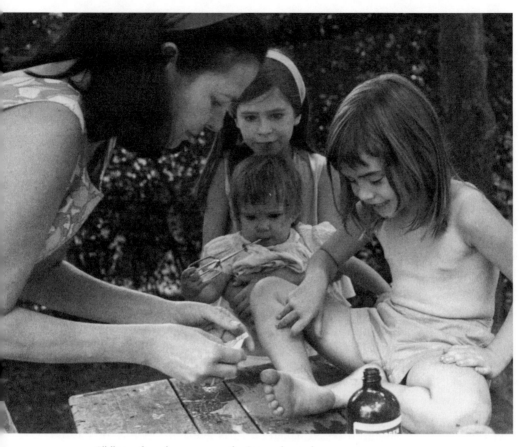

Siblings often share one another's growing pains.

are situations when run-of-the-mill rivalry escalates to serious, possibly dangerous aggression.

Besides rivalry, there are other, more unusual, situations that can cause a family greater stress than do the average growing pains. Having a brother or sister who suffers from a serious illness or disability poses unique problems that can be especially difficult for children and adolescents. Siblings who are involved in a sexual relationship with each other can suffer guilt and shame in the short term, as well as significant emotional, psychological, and even physical damage over time. Finally, the death of a loved one may evoke confusion, anger, loneliness, depression—all of which are common among children or adolescents who lose a brother or sister.

The following sections introduce each of these special situations in which sibling relationships may become troubling. For the purposes of this book, the word *siblings* refers to any children who grow up in the same family, whether or not they have the same birth parents. They can be half-brothers and half-sisters, stepchildren, foster children, or adopted children.

SIBLING AGGRESSION

By the time we reach adolescence, most of us are familiar with sibling rivalry. Sisters and brothers argue, fight, and very often come to blows. It is an inevitable part of sibling relationships. Most often rivalry occurs over a family role, a parent's attention, a friend, or even a toy. Despite the seemingly eternal tension, more often than not siblings grow up to have close, loving relationships.

But mere rivalry is not the only kind of conflict between siblings. There are many who take their aggression to extremes, escalating what may have started as harmless quarreling until it becomes excessive violence and exploitation. Such situations can lead to emotional and psychological problems in the brother or sister who has been victimized. Although it might seem likely that parents or some other authority figure would be on hand to prevent the aggression from getting out of control, many cases of abusive sibling relationships are hidden from the rest of the family.

Studies have revealed that some brothers and sisters not only beat each other up, but also use knives, guns, or other weapons to threaten or attack each other. Experts in the field are especially concerned because sibling aggression has been occurring more frequently than all other forms of family violence.

SIBLING ILLNESS OR DISABILITY

There are approximately 18 million disabled children and adolescents in the United States. Nearly one in ten children under 18 years of age suffers from a physical disability or chronic disease. Are the siblings of these children at greater risk than the general population for emotional and behavioral problems? Much research indicates that the answer is yes, especially for adolescents.

Traditionally, little attention has been paid to the needs of siblings of people with a mental illness or disability. That is in the process of changing, with the emergence of publicized personal accounts by siblings and population studies by professionals. The unique reality of each situation

Having a brother or sister with a disability can make a youngster's life "special" in many ways—some good, some painful.

is determined by the personal qualities of the siblings and the circumstances of their lives. Nevertheless, there are some general methods of dealing with these problems, and we will explore them in Chapter 4.

SIBLING INCEST

When most of us think of incest, we think of a father sexually abusing his daughter. This is considered *parental incest,* a term also applied to sexual contact between stepfather and daughter, father and son, stepfather and son, mother and son, stepmother and son, mother and daughter, and stepmother and daughter. The father-daughter type has received the most attention and is the most frequently reported.

But there is another category of incest, involving siblings. Sibling incest can occur between brother and sister, brother and brother, and sister and sister. Personal accounts and case studies generally point to the offender as male and the victim as female. It is true that the most common type of sibling incest is between brother and sister. However, it's important to remember that there are also cases of girls sexually abusing their younger brothers and sisters.

We should make clear what we do *not* mean by incest. Most, if not all, children go through a brief period of sexual comparison and exploration in early childhood. This period of sex play involves a group of young children around the same age who are mutually curious about their bodies. They may express their curiosity by showing and touching genitals, much as they might show and touch navels. When this occurs between siblings, it is not considered incest, but rather a healthy and normal part of growing up.

Incest among brothers and sisters, on the other hand, is a different type of sexual contact. Usually it is an abusive and manipulative power play initiated by one sibling against another. When force is not necessary, often it is because the younger sibling does not fully understand what is going on. As Heidi Vanderbilt wrote in a 1992 article on the subject, incest "is a violation of the child where he or she lives—literally and metaphorically. A child molested by a stranger can run home for help and comfort. A victim of incest cannot."

DEATH OF A SIBLING

When a child's brother or sister dies, the surviving sibling "loses a friend, playmate, confidant, role model, and lifelong companion," according to Buz and Joanie Overbeck, authors of *Helping Children Cope with Loss*. And for the parents, "the loss of a child is often so traumatic that they have little left to give to the surviving children."

Many people assume that children under eight or nine years of age are incapable of understanding the finality of death. But in a study of young children by T. P. Reilly and colleagues, the majority of the girls and boys in the sample had some understanding of their own mortality by the age of six. Although very young children are less likely to comprehend the full impact of death, they still feel some sense of loss when a sibling dies.

If the sibling who died was older, surviving brothers and sisters tend to have more difficulty recovering than they do from the death of a younger child. And siblings who lose a brother or sister they have never seen—as when a baby dies at birth—find it hard to experience the death as real. Although the particulars may change from one family to another, psychologists and family therapists believe that many children suffer significant emotional problems when a brother or sister dies.

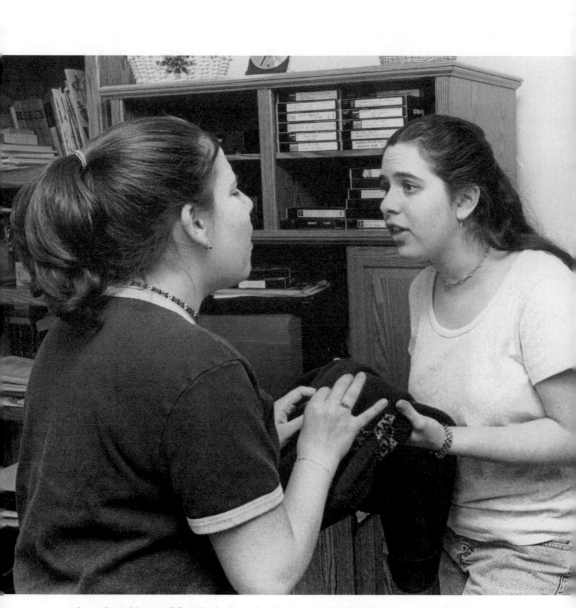

Throughout history, sibling rivalry has often been considered natural. But when does typical conflict cross the line into aggression?

2

SIBLING RELATIONAL PROBLEMS: A HISTORY

During the late 19th and early 20th centuries, Sigmund Freud, often referred to as the father of psychoanalysis, explored the effects of childhood experiences on his patients. His research attempted to determine how earlier traumatic experiences might affect a person's later psychological and emotional condition. Freud coined the term *psychic trauma* to describe this progression, and his work helped establish the idea that many adult neuroses have their roots in childhood problems.

Although Freud's theories were often debated at the time, psychiatric professionals ever since have repeatedly treated people who were struggling to cope with traumas experienced in childhood. Among these traumas, problems in sibling relationships have been gaining more and more attention.

SIBLING AGGRESSION

Conflict between brothers and sisters has always existed. Even the ancients knew that sometimes sibling aggression can get out of hand. In Roman mythology, for example, Romulus and Remus, twin brothers who supposedly founded the city of Rome, quarreled with one another, and Romulus killed his brother. But throughout history, sibling conflicts have generally been viewed simply as minor hurdles in the process of growing up and learning to interact socially.

Today, sibling rivalry is still commonly seen as normal. However, more attention is being paid to the unhealthy aggression and abusive relationships that can warp a person's ability to function throughout life. Since the 1970s the topic has been taken seriously enough to encourage systematic research. In 1971 M. Bard published a review of New York's 1965 crime statistics, showing that 3 percent of all homicides were sibling murders. As startling as that fact may be, it was considered an aberration—a rare occurrence—at the time. But

In the legend of Romulus and Remus, the twin boys are thrown into a river by a wicked uncle and rescued by a herdsman. This 17th-century engraving shows the herdsman carrying one of the boys home to his wife. The twins grew up to become the founders of Rome, the legend says—but when they had a falling out, Romulus murdered Remus.

it is likely that many other serious, yet nonfatal, incidents were going unreported and undiscovered, and this may still be true today.

SIBLING ILLNESS OR DISABILITY

Up through the 1950s and 1960s, traditional methods of therapy often fostered negative assumptions about mental illness or physical disability. In fact, family members seeking treatment were often held accountable in some way for the problem, or at least they were made to feel it was shameful. As a result, many of those who did enter therapy walked away feeling even more afraid and confused than before.

During recent decades, society's opinions have started to change. People have become more aware of the problems of long-term disability and mental illness, and the associated feelings of shame have diminished to some degree. The change has been spurred in part by several pieces of legislation that have brought disability into public awareness.

In 1975, the federal Education for All Handicapped Children Act became law. Since revised, and renamed the Individuals with Disabilities Education Act (IDEA), the law orders states to provide disabled children with "a free, appropriate public education." Ever since the enactment of IDEA, many boys and girls have attended school with disabled classmates—exposure their parents and grandparents probably did not have. These children are more likely to grow up realizing that persons with disabilities are just like everyone else in almost every way.

Subsequent laws have strengthened the rights of disabled individuals and their families. For instance, the Americans with Disabilities Act, passed in 1990, makes it illegal for employers, companies that provide public transportation, and other public entities to discriminate against people on the basis of mental or physical disability. Such legislation has helped those with disabilities, along with their siblings and parents. Nevertheless, the disabled still encounter prejudice and sometimes ridicule in their day-to-day lives, and these problems can add to the difficulties faced by their siblings.

SIBLING INCEST

Though it cannot be precisely documented, incest between siblings has most likely always existed—just as other types of incest have. And it has almost always been socially forbidden.

Much of the original research into the causes and effects of incest was conducted by Sigmund Freud. In "The Aetiology of Hysteria," published

SIBLING RELATIONAL PROBLEMS IN THE BIBLE

T o understand how important our ancestors considered sibling relations, we need look no further than the Bible. The Old Testament contains many examples of problems involving siblings, ranging from jealousy to incest and murder.

In the biblical account, sibling struggles begin with the world's first children, Cain and Abel, sons of Adam and Eve. Cain grows up to be a farmer, Abel a shepherd. At one point they both make offerings to God. Abel's sacrifice of lambs is approved by the Lord, but Cain's offering of "fruit of the ground" is not. Cain grows jealous and kills Abel. Asked by God to account for Abel's absence, Cain feigns ignorance, adding the immortal line, "Am I my brother's keeper?" The deception fails, of course, and Cain is banished for his crime.

Many generations later, the theme is replayed in the story of Jacob and Esau. Twin sons of Isaac and Rebekah, the boys are born so close together that Jacob emerges from the womb holding on to Esau's heel. As the first-born, though, Esau holds a birthright, that is, the right to inherit his father's property and become head of the family. But one day when Esau comes in starving from the field, he asks Jacob for food, and before feeding him, Jacob makes him relinquish his birthright. Later, when their father is dying, Jacob pretends to be Esau and gets the patriarchal blessing—with its promise of future prosperity—that the father intended for the older brother. Furious, Esau decides to kill Jacob, but Jacob flees. Years later, when the two brothers meet, they reconcile; still, it is Jacob, renamed Israel, who becomes the founder of the Jewish people.

Perhaps appropriately, Jacob soon has to contend with sibling rivalry in his own household. By an act of trickery he is induced to marry Leah when he prefers her younger sister, Rachel; then he marries Rachel as well, and the two sisters compete jealously for his affections. Their rivalry carries over to their children. Joseph, a son of Rachel's, becomes Jacob's favorite child. Naturally this makes Joseph's half-brothers angry, and they sell him into slavery. Afterwards, they tear up the "coat of many colors" that his father gave him, dip it in goat's blood, and send it to Jacob as a sign that the boy has been killed by wild beasts. Only one brother, Reuben, expresses grief and dismay. Again, however, the story turns out well when Joseph becomes powerful in Egypt and reunites the family.

All of these narratives are found in the Book of Genesis. Later in the Old

Testament, in II Samuel, the theme reappears with some new complications. Absalom and Amnon, sons of King David, have a sister named Tamar, with whom Amnon falls in love. When Amnon tries to seduce Tamar, she rejects him, and then he rapes her. Absalom, learning what has happened, has his servants murder his brother. But the avenging Absalom eventually loses his own life in a revolt against his father.

Love and hate, companionship and jealousy, joy and grief—all of these paradoxes of sibling relationships appear not only in the Bible, but in other ancient religious texts, legends, and epics as well. They have always been part and parcel of the human experience.

in 1896, Freud identified childhood sexual abuse as the cause of much mental and emotional illness in adulthood.

More than a decade later, having developed his research further, Freud asserted in *Totem and Taboo* that humans are innately incestuous—that is, people have a built-in impulse toward incest. We resist sex-

Sigmund Freud, one of the founders of modern psychiatry, believed that humans have a built-in impulse toward incest that is controlled by society and culture.

Because grief is generally a private matter in Western societies, young people faced with the death of a sibling have often received little guidance except from their own families.

ual relations with family members, Freud said, only because of cultural and social pressures. His views were founded on a widely accepted assumption that animals, including our own primitive ancestors, mated with blood relatives.

Around the same time, the Finnish anthropologist Edward Westermarck countered Freud's theories. Westermarck proposed that individuals who live in very close proximity during early childhood develop a secure bond, causing them to have an innate aversion to sexual intercourse with each other. On the other hand, if that early bonding never takes place—because of separation, divorce, or another reason—incest may occur between siblings. He called his theory *incest avoidance*.

Widely rejected during his lifetime, Westermarck's thinking has recently been recognized as an important contribution to the study of incest and why it occurs. Subsequent experiments with primates and other species have supported his views.

DEATH OF A SIBLING

To trace the history of how brothers and sisters—or any individuals, for that matter—have handled the death of a loved one is mostly guesswork. To this day, grief is treated as a very private matter, and little or no training on how to deal with it is available.

Children learn how to respond to death from their parents and society. If both those sources show that expressing one's fears, loneliness, and hurt is a positive response, then children will open up and let the emotions flow. Conversely, if adults mourn by shoving the tears back and keeping their feelings to themselves—the common response in many (not all) nations in the northern half of the world—then children tend to follow suit.

Until the last two decades there has been a great void in therapy and counseling designed for grief. Recently, however, several organizations have emerged that attempt to address the problem. One of them, the Grief Recovery Institute, was founded by two men who grew frustrated in their own search for help in getting over the death of several loved ones. The institute has now established outreach programs all over the United States and Canada. (See Appendix: For More Information.)

Sibling aggression often has its roots in resentment over the birth of a new child.

3

SIBLING AGGRESSION

For most children, especially firstborns, the arrival of a new brother or sister is a cause of considerable distress. No longer are Mommy and Daddy exclusively theirs; from that point on, they must struggle to keep their parents' attention.

It is important to realize, however, that this basic kind of sibling rivalry is entirely normal and natural. "Most parents think that kids are supposed to love each other, but they don't," says Cathleen Brown, a clinical psychologist. "The fighting will happen no matter what parents do."

Early on, resentment of a brother or sister can result in excessive crying, problems with toilet training, demands for attention, and other negative and regressive behavior. Later, the sibling rivalry can take the form of open or subtle conflict with the brother or sister. The subject of this chapter is what can happen when the rivalry turns into outright aggression—which, in extreme and rare cases, can include efforts to cause serious physical harm by poisoning or the breaking of bones, or even attempts to murder the sibling.

In the majority of reported cases of sibling aggression, an older child has abused a younger, smaller brother or sister. This does not mean, however, that older siblings are the more aggressive, at least not physically. Typically, younger siblings, who have not yet been socialized to restrain themselves, are actually more violent than their older sisters and brothers. In one early study, dating from 1960, H. L. Koch surveyed 360 five- to six-year-old children with one sibling. The parents of these children reported that 28.4 percent engaged in severe and frequent quarreling, 36 percent in moderate quarreling, and 35.5 percent in very rare altercations.

Fortunately, a small child who throws punches at an older, bigger sibling is not likely to cause serious injury. And most such violent acts occur less frequently as the child grows older. That is, as children mature, they normally progress to less physical forms of conflict. Some siblings, however, continue to

Moderate quarreling between young sisters or brothers is commonplace.

be physically abusive, and they may keep their tactics hidden from their parents and other adults. A study by M. A. Straus and colleagues looked at 2,143 families, of which 733 had at least two children between the ages of three and 17 living at home. This study revealed a number of disturbing acts committed by brothers and sisters against each other. Over the course of one year, 117 beat up a sibling, six threatened a sibling with a knife or gun, and two actually used a knife or gun.

In a study of seven- to eight-year-olds by A. M. Minnett and colleagues, aggression was found to be stronger when the siblings were closer in age. But regardless of age difference, children tend to perceive older siblings of the same sex as more dominating than those of the opposite sex. In general, too, brothers are more aggressive with brothers, and sisters with sisters.

Boys are more likely to use physical force to solve conflicts, whereas girls tend toward a strategy of ignoring the sibling. But both boys and girls use various forms of yelling and ignoring more often than physical force.

WHAT CAUSES SIBLING AGGRESSION?

Aggressiveness is a large part of interaction between brothers and sisters. Healthy conflict, though it may seem unfriendly, is still a showing of feelings. In that sense, sibling aggression can serve as an acceptable outlet for frustration. Children cannot hit or attack the parent or teacher who makes them angry, so they lash out at an equal, a sibling. Hurting a sister or brother may bring some sense of relief from fear or frustration.

For children and adolescents who have a turbulent home life, physical sibling rivalry can be a source of stability. Their fighting is familiar and consistent. For them, some comfort can be found in having a routine battle with a brother or sister.

Boys are more likely than girls to use physical force in their sibling conflicts.

PARENTS AND FAMILY CONDITIONS

Mothers and fathers, of course, have a great deal to do with their children's tendency toward sibling aggression. Parents who are rarely available, either physically or emotionally, are more likely to have children who are overly aggressive with each other than are parents who are regularly on hand to supervise and help resolve conflicts. When parents are generally uninterested and emotionally absent, children may behave aggressively out of a desperate attempt to get attention.

Various family conditions that can reduce parents' attentiveness toward the children also tend to heighten sibling conflict. For instance, aggression between brothers and sisters seems to increase as family size increases. And as Michael Kahn and Genevieve Monks report, research indicates that alcoholic parents—who are often unavailable

Abusive siblings often come from a home in which the parents have frequent arguments.

emotionally—can cause serious damage to the sibling relationship by increasing sibling rivalry. Rivalry among brothers and sisters—so common in mild forms—can reach violent and exploitative extremes in an alcoholic family. Or, parents with eating disorders may be so threatened by the relationship between their sons and daughters that they discourage sibling bonding and intimacy; in these cases, conflict and aggression are the likely results.

Other case studies have shown that highly abusive siblings have mothers and fathers who, if not divorced or separated, are frequently arguing or in conflict with each other. Not surprisingly, parents who abuse each other or their children set the unhealthy example of solving problems with aggression, and their sons and daughters are all too capable of imitating them. A study by P. Crittenden, published in *Child Abuse and Neglect*, found that children as young as two showed the same patterns of interaction (good or bad) with their younger siblings as their mothers did with them.

■　　　■　　　■

Juan's story, reported by A. H. Green in 1994, is a case in point. At age 10 Juan went to live with his mother and her boyfriend. For the seven years before that, he had lived with his father and stepmother. On a number of occasions his father had beaten him on the head and burned him with an iron.

When he moved into his mother's house, Juan met his two younger half-brothers, and soon he was showing a great deal of resentment toward them. He hit them quite a few times. He also became hyperactive and aggressive at school and at home. Within about a year, his aggression reached the dangerous stage—he forced his three-year-old half-brother to drink lye.

When taken to a child therapist, Juan talked about some of the things he enjoyed doing. For instance, he said he liked to catch mice and drop them in boiling water. Or he liked to smash mice on the head with a hammer and flush them down the toilet. The therapist asked why he liked to behave this way, and Juan responded by showing burn marks on his shoulder and other scars on his scalp. "This is what my father did to me," he said.

■　　　■　　　■

Clearly Juan had learned from his father that physical violence was the way to handle stressful situations. Thus, the boy dealt with his jeal-

SIBLING RIVALRY: FAMILY PREVENTIVE MEASURES

The literature on sibling rivalry and aggression is full of wise tips about ways for families to deal with conflicts among brothers and sisters. The goal is to prevent ordinary sibling rivalry from becoming severe or damaging to the children. Here are a few such ideas:

- Be sure each child gets ample one-on-one time with each parent. Show him or her that there is plenty of love for everyone in the family.

- Assure each child of his or her uniqueness and specialness.

- When complimenting one child, compliment the siblings as well.

- Don't compare children to one another.

One way to reduce sibling rivalry is to show children that there is plenty of love available for everyone in the family.

- Remember that a certain amount of sibling rivalry is normal.
- Ordinary bickering can safely be ignored. But if it continues for a long while, investigate the source of the conflict.
- Distinguish between play fighting (that is, roughhousing by mutual consent) and real fighting.
- In deciding whether and how to intervene in siblings' fights, take into account not only the degree of violence, but also the ages and relative sizes of the siblings.
- As you help siblings resolve their differences, take the opportunity to teach them social skills so they can learn to avoid fights in the future.

ousy and his perceived loss of his mother's attention by attacking their cause: his new siblings. Naturally, a child who has been abused by a parent grows up viewing aggression as not only normal but also necessary to prove one's power. Juan's case shows how readily patterns of violence can be handed down from one generation to the next.

A number of researchers have looked at connections between a child's abuse by a parent and later violent activity. In 1996, for example, J. Haapasalo and T. Hämäläinen reported a study of 89 prison inmates between the ages of 16 and 22. Among these young people, 86.5 percent of the violent offenders (those convicted of murder, rape, or similarly violent crimes), as well as 78.4 percent of the property offenders (those convicted of crimes such as burglary or theft), had been physically abused as children.

It is important to remember, though, that parental abuse and rejection do not directly *cause* either sibling aggression or later criminal activity. They merely increase the chances that they will occur. Other factors—such as a child's personality, interaction with caring adults, and community involvement—can bring about a more positive future for victims of child abuse.

PUNISHMENT AND DISCIPLINE

Punishment also appears to play a role in the extent to which siblings fight. Regardless of who started a fight, older children are more likely than their younger siblings to be blamed for the conflict. Because of this

Consistent parental discipline helps control aggressive behavior between siblings.

pattern, according to a study by R. B. Felson and N. Russo conducted in 1988, it is not uncommon for younger siblings to initiate aggression on subsequent occasions. Why not? They learned from their parents that they were not responsible for fighting with their older siblings.

Another factor is the consistency with which parents punish their children for inappropriate actions. If parents sometimes threaten to punish aggressive behavior but don't follow through, children learn to ignore the threats and are likely to solve more and more conflicts with abuse.

THE ROLE OF SOCIETY

Although many people believe that aggression is simply a fundamental part of human nature, others feel that the root cause of individual aggressiveness—especially among teenagers—is the violence in our society at large. Many point to the steady rise in violent crime, including abuses against the disabled and children, in the United States and Canada. This, they say, is a reflection of society's attitudes toward aggression. If adults cannot control their own behavior, they certainly cannot prevent aggression among their children.

The prevalence of violence in the mass media also comes under attack. If our movies and television shows commonly portray violence—often in glamorous ways—why should we be surprised when children imitate what they see? Media influence is a tangled and difficult subject, but many social critics believe it is involved in the problem of aggression in one way or another.

Some observers also point to the proliferation of single-parent homes, in which boys in particular may rebel against an overinvolved single mother—presumably to prove their manliness. Relatively easy and unmonitored access to alcohol and other drugs is also seen as a contributing factor.

In addition to taking some of the blame for fostering sibling aggression, society must endure some of the effects of this aggression. K. J. Gully and colleagues studied extreme sibling aggression to explore how it contributed to later violent behavior. The findings revealed that those who initiated violence against siblings in childhood and adolescence were more likely to be involved in violent crimes as adults. They were also more likely to engage in abusive relationships. Thus, it is not only family members who pay the price for serious sibling aggression. Society as a whole suffers in the long run.

TREATMENT OPTIONS

When severe conflicts between siblings cannot be resolved by parents, counseling may be the next step. Therapy sessions often entail teaching one or more of the children how to negotiate and work out their differences in a less destructive manner. If repeated conflicts are based on a more deep-seated problem, intense therapy may be necessary.

The most violent cases of serious aggression may end up in court. If treatment fails or is not forthcoming soon enough, an abuser may ultimately be punished instead of treated.

SIBLING MURDER: THE DARKEST SIDE OF AGGRESSION

I t is very rare, of course, for siblings to let their rivalry go so far that one deliberately kills another. Still, this extreme behavior has always been acknowledged as a possibility, as shown by the biblical account of Cain and Abel.

In 1994 the U.S. Department of Justice concluded that sibling homicide accounted for approximately 1.5 percent of all homicides—quite a small percentage, considering how many opportunities siblings have to get angry at one another. Yet many criminologists believe that figure is too low, because some sibling homicides may well be classified as accidental deaths. If a young boy falls down a stairway and breaks his neck, no one may ever know that his older brother pushed him. Even if the parents do know, they are unlikely to report that fact to authorities. It would not be unusual if the parents cared more about protecting their family and their remaining children than about punishing the young perpetrator.

The potential conflict between parents and the justice system was highlighted by a 1998 case in California. According to authorities, a 14-year-old middle-class boy developed such jealousy and hatred toward his 12-year-old sister that he recruited two friends to help him kill her. One night, they stabbed her nine times while she slept.

When the boys were arrested, two of them confessed to the murder. At the court hearing, however, all three pleaded not guilty, claiming the confessions had been coerced by the police. Meanwhile the boys' parents—including the parents of the slain girl—insisted that their sons were innocent of any crime. Worried that the boys weren't being fed properly, the parents even brought food to the courtroom for them.

In cases of real or suspected sibling murder, the parents who have lost one child stand to lose another if the accused is sent to jail. And they will suffer the shame of having reared a murderer. It's no wonder that they do everything they can to avoid the charge.

The Bible's account of Cain killing Abel shows that sibling murder, though rare, has always been part of human history.

A long-term disability like Down syndrome can have a psychological impact not only on the child who has it but also on the other children in the family.

4

SIBLING ILLNESS OR DISABILITY

For a child, having a seriously disabled or ill sister or brother is not necessarily a psychologically damaging experience. In fact, spending time caring for such a sibling can teach a child to be nurturing and sensitive to others' needs. As a result of the added responsibility, many individuals in this situation mature much earlier than their peers.

Overall, most children and adolescents with ill siblings do not suffer greater psychological problems than those with healthy siblings. Some do, however, and they are the subject of this chapter.

Siblings who live daily with the illness or disability of a brother or sister are likely to find their own energy for coping with normal development depleted. In fact, their maturation may be disrupted from the moment the problem appears in their family. This is especially true for adolescents. Adolescence can be a particularly difficult time. This is when teenagers are trying to establish their own sense of identity, as they attempt to define who they are and how they fit into the world. This is the time when they begin to come to terms with intimacy and sexuality, seek independence from their family, and make decisions about continuing education and careers. The illness or disability of a brother or sister is likely to affect all these issues.

Siblings of an ill child often experience intense feelings of anger. The anger may be directed at God or at fate for the unanticipated family tragedy. Sometimes it is turned on the parents whose energy is consumed by the child with the illness or disability. Or it may be directed at the ill sibling—for disrupting family life or for not getting better. And sometimes the anger is turned inward, when children sense their inability to protect and rescue someone they love.

Conditions that develop or reveal themselves over time—for instance, pervasive developmental disorder, schizophrenia, and bipolar disorder—can also cause siblings to feel a sense of loss. The healthy siblings mourn for the brother or sister they knew and loved before the onset of the disease. They may also grieve for the loss of normal family life.

Some siblings strive to become "perfect" children who can compensate their overburdened parents for the problems of the ill child. In this case, they may deny themselves healthy opportunities for rebellion. They may also experience a form of survivor's guilt for having been spared a similar illness or disability, and this may intensify their desire to prove their invulnerability and competence.

On the other hand, having an ill or disabled brother or sister may bring on feelings of social inadequacy or depression. The children who are well may resent the ill sibling because of the extra attention he or she gets from their parents. They may feel that they are being left to fend for themselves or that they are unfairly burdened with added responsibilities, such as caring for younger siblings or doing more household chores. They may generally feel unappreciated by others. At the same time, they may feel guilty for harboring such resentments.

It is also not uncommon for healthy siblings to experience extreme anxiety and loneliness, because they think no one could possibly know how they feel. Even if they are frustrated or lonely, they may hide these feelings from parents and teachers who could help. Researchers J. V. Lavigne and M. Ryan found that siblings of ill or disabled children tend to be more socially withdrawn and irritable than children with healthy siblings. At school, siblings of disabled children tend to be more aggressive in their interaction with peers and may seek attention by being disruptive in class.

On the whole, there seem to be some differences between brothers and sisters in the way they react to ill or disabled siblings. Sisters seem to spend more time taking care of the disabled sibling. And the more disabled the sibling, the more responsibility the well sister must take on—a situation that often results in a less intimate relationship between them. On the positive side, some research suggests that certain older sisters actually derive a sense of satisfaction from nurturing their younger siblings. In many families with a disabled or ill child, the one who seems to suffer the most is the younger brother. He is less likely to be a caretaker, and he tends to demand more attention from the parents.

In general, brothers and sisters who are close in age to their ill or disabled sibling tend to experience more personal conflict about their relationships than those who are further apart in age. Siblings who are much older, in particular, are more comfortable and satisfied with their

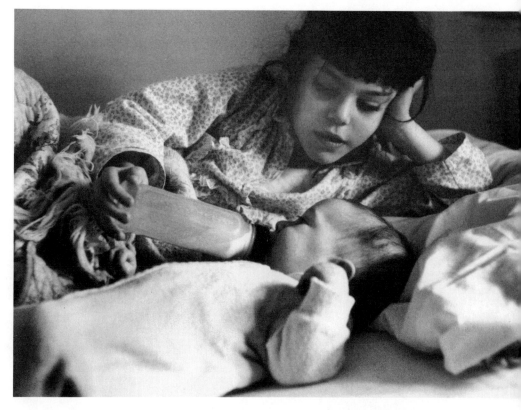

Compared to brothers, sisters tend to spend more time caring for a sibling with an illness or disability.

interaction with a younger disabled brother or sister. The ways in which well siblings demonstrate their conflicted feelings also differ according to age. For example, preschoolers tend to withdraw and become irritable, whereas older children are likely to be socially disruptive.

EFFECTS OF PARTICULAR CONDITIONS

Some studies have focused on the effects of specific illnesses or disabilities. This research tends to show that, for the healthy siblings, different illnesses can foster different problems.

DOWN SYNDROME AND PERVASIVE DEVELOPMENTAL DISORDER

In 1996 S. Fisman and colleagues published the results of a three-year study that examined healthy siblings (between the ages of 8 and 16) of

A girl with Down syndrome plays a board game with her brother. Down syndrome causes different degrees of mental retardation, from mild to severe.

children with either Down syndrome (DS) or pervasive developmental disorder (PDD). The researchers compared these groups with siblings of healthy children. Children with DS are born with an extra chromosome that causes certain physical characteristics—floppy muscles, slanted eyes, a nose with a very flat bridge—and varying degrees of mental retardation. DS can be diagnosed at birth, and it can range from mild to severe. PDD, on the other hand, may not be apparent in newborns. It develops over time, causing afflicted children to become more demanding and less able to adapt to change as they mature.

Generally, the Fisman study found that DS is less disruptive than PDD. Siblings of children with DS had fewer problems in school and didn't seem to internalize their emotions as much as did siblings of children with PDD. Because PDD often involves a gradual decline and a lot of uncertainty, siblings (and parents) tend to endure high levels of stress that can lead to psychological and behavioral problems. Unfortunately, one of the characteristics of children with PDD is that they may not understand or be able to show certain emotions. This may lead their siblings to keep their own emotions inside. Interestingly, however, siblings of children with DS and PDD reported less conflict and more warmth in their family relationships than did siblings from families with no disabled members.

OTHER CONDITIONS

A number of studies support the finding that particular diseases or disabilities can evoke different types of reactions in well siblings. For example, research by K. A. Roeder indicates that siblings of psychiatrically hospitalized adolescents often suffer from lower self-esteem and greater ego problems than do their peers. Other studies show that children and teenagers whose siblings are seriously emotionally disturbed may fear "catching" the illness. Even if they know it cannot be contagious, some adolescents—all of whom are dealing with their own identity concerns—may worry about developing mental illness themselves. Or they may become anxious about being viewed as just like their sick sibling. According to Lavigne and Ryan, such concerns can cause antisocial behavior, often directed at the children's parents and teachers. Or, as D. T. Marsh points out, the well children may develop a desire to become ill, partly because they sense that their parents value the sick sibling more.

Siblings of mentally ill children often remain walled off in their own anguish and confusion. Unless they are involved in a support group, they may not be aware that their experiences are shared by many other young people. Or they may not understand that their sibling's mental illness has a great impact on their own lives. Their parents, whose energy may be consumed in meeting the needs of the child with mental illness, may have little sense of the turmoil that exists below the surface.

In addition to the emotional burden, many day-to-day demands confront siblings of mentally ill children. Their world inside and outside the family is likely to be transformed by the presence of mental illness. Siblings must cope with the sometimes volatile behavior of their brother or sister. This may involve hostility, abuse, or assault; mood swings and unpredictability; socially offensive or embarrassing behavior; and the inability to relate to others emotionally or otherwise.

UNDERLYING FACTORS

Certainly, each situation is different, depending on the type of disability or illness, the family, and the siblings themselves. Yet there are some underlying factors that can increase or reduce the likelihood that problems will develop between well and ill siblings.

For example, if one child is severely disabled or suffering from a terminal illness, the parents, especially the mother, may become overstressed to the point of not being able to "be there" for the other children. This may be because the disabled or sick child's demands make the parents more irritable, so they lash out at the other children. Or perhaps the emotional stress leads to severe depression in the parents. Whatever the reason, healthy siblings suffer, and they may vent their pain by physically acting out or by suppressing their feelings. If not resolved, these problems can become overwhelming as the healthy sibling moves from puberty through adolescence into adulthood.

Generally, the less a family communicates and encourages expression of feelings, the more likely children are to suppress their thoughts and emotions. Ultimately, those thoughts and feelings will come out, often being expressed in negative ways toward the disabled sibling.

Other family factors have been identified as contributing to the problems surrounding illness and disability. Although these difficulties know no economic boundaries, research has revealed that lower-class families tend to endure more stress, largely because they can afford fewer outlets to relieve it. Also, according to A. Gath, M. Seligman, and other researchers, siblings from smaller families may feel a greater strain, simply because their fewer numbers mean that a larger workload is given to each child.

Just as family factors can make the situation worse, they can also improve the outlook for healthy siblings. Adolescents who have a strong support system—in the form of their parents, other relatives, close friends, church, or community—are much better able to handle the psychological and emotional strain of interacting with a sick or disabled sibling. In the study of DS and PDD, the brothers and sisters—especially, those of children with DS—adjusted more easily when their parents were happily married, experienced little depression, and handled stress well. Any of these ameliorating factors will help make the well sibling less vulnerable to developmental problems, enabling him or her to grow up with a healthy perspective.

Personality also plays a large role in how the sibling manages. According to Fisman and colleagues, if the child or adolescent begins with a good disposition and high self-esteem, the difficulties involved with a sick sister or brother are less daunting. And the more positive and secure the sibling feels, the more likely a positive relationship will develop between the children.

THE ROLE OF SOCIETY

Despite changes in attitudes in recent decades, society tends to segregate and ostracize people with a mental or physical disability. For sib-

One child's illness or disability may make parents more short-tempered with their other children.

lings, the social stigma of having an "abnormal" family can be very debilitating, corroding their confidence during social interaction. Children and teens, especially, tend to have difficulty dealing with the reactions of others to their disabled brother or sister, particularly when the sibling's behavior is considered socially offensive. They are embarrassed because they are "different" by association.

A success-oriented society like ours devalues those who can't meet high standards, and it often defines dependence on others as moral failure. This inclination to pass judgment stems from an ignorance about disabilities and a fear of catching the mental or physical illness, as if it were contagious. Again, as with aggression, the mass media are partially to blame, because they often portray disabilities in unrealistic, frightening, and disparaging ways. Unfortunately, family members not only feel hurt by the stigma, but they may also internalize it so much that they, too, believe it.

As mentioned in Chapter 2, the Americans with Disabilities Act of 1990 now protects persons with disabilities from discrimination in employment and public services. Nevertheless, stigmatization remains a pervasive problem for both the afflicted and their families.

TREATMENT OPTIONS

Some siblings may join with their families in trying to avoid their anguish by hiding behind a facade of normalcy. But this denial of deeper problems only undermines the youngsters' ability to resolve them and increases the amount of unfinished business they carry into adulthood. To deal with the situation, family members need to take active steps, either at home or, in more severe cases, through the help of outside agencies.

OPTIONS WITHIN THE FAMILY SETTING

When attempting to come to terms with the loss of a so-called normal sibling to illness or disability, the more family members educate themselves about the condition and discuss it with comforting others, the more confident and less anxious they will be. J. Itzkowitz suggests these other steps that parents can take:

- Give the well sibling information about the brother's or sister's health condition.
- Treat the well child as a child, not as an adult caretaker.

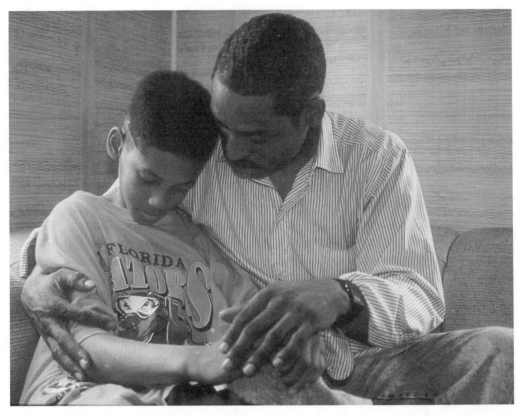

Parents and relatives play a crucial role in helping youngsters cope with the emotional burdens of having an ill or disabled sibling.

- Ask for and value the healthy child's opinions, and include him or her in family decision making.

OPTIONS OUTSIDE THE FAMILY

In addition to getting support from parents, relatives, friends, and neighbors—especially those who have been through a similar situation—siblings can turn to books, audio and video cassettes, and other literature to provide inspiration, hope, and valuable information. For those who may not get the comfort and answers they need from these sources, support groups are an important option. They offer siblings a safe haven for discussing their fears, resolving emotional burdens, and getting essential information about the disability or illness and its treatment. Ideally, the group will help children and teens develop realistic

WHAT THE SIBLINGS SAY

Joan Fleitas, a professor of nursing at Fairfield University, has established a World Wide Web site called *Band-Aides and Blackboards* that focuses on "growing up with medical problems" (see Appendix: For More Information). Along with a great deal of other information, the site offers stories by siblings of children with serious illnesses or disabilities. Here are some excerpts from what the children have to say:

An older sister of a young child with a severe neurological disorder:

Endless hours of screaming and crying is enough to make anyone crazy . . . and Reba did that for over six months. We used to take turns walking with her around the house, singing to her, doing our best to try to calm her down. Nothing worked! I got mad, upset, angry, hateful and resentful of her and of my family. It wasn't fair!

A sister of a boy with leukemia:

Alexis used to get really big packages so I used to get very jealous. Wouldn't you? But over the year I got used to everybody feeling bad for him, and giving him so much attention. In some ways, I actually got something out of it, too.

A nine-year-old boy:

Tonight Dad was telling me how hard it was when Trudy was in the hospital. He doesn't think it was hard for me at all. . . . Sometimes I feel so alone and left out and even unloved.

A girl whose brother has been sick since he was six and she was four:

Lots of times Kyle had to stay at the hospital and I couldn't see him or my Mom. That made me very sad. . . . When Kyle is sick and he needs help, then he gets more attention from our parents. Sometimes that makes me feel angry and frustrated. . . . There are good things and bad things about being the sibling of a sick kid. Sometimes I would like to have a different brother who is not sick. But I don't want to send Kyle away. I love him with all my heart.

expectations about life with their siblings, and it will guide them in figuring out how to balance their own lives.

Support group sessions may be led by family members, professional therapists, or a combination of the two. In cases of mental illness, organizations like the National Alliance for the Mentally Ill (see Appendix: For More Information) can provide lists of local support groups.

If family members or a support group still leave siblings feeling desperate, brief individual counseling may be beneficial. According to experts like D. T. Marsh and R. Dickens, signs that indicate a need for therapy include sharp mood swings, difficulty deriving any pleasure from life, and the inability to control intense anger at family members or at oneself. Generally, personal therapy is for those who feel demoralized or seriously depressed, or who suffer severe anxiety, panic, or fear.

Professional counseling should help the sibling attain more effective methods of coping with the illness or disability. It should also reduce the level of distress and help the person feel more positive about him- or herself and the future. Therapy can range from brief, less intensive and less supportive forms to intensive psychotherapy. The latter is more appropriate for siblings who, despite other kinds of support, still endure severe and deep-seated problems.

Sibling incest, because it is considered shameful, is often kept secret. But having no one to talk to intensifies the young person's pain.

5

SIBLING INCEST

Sexual contact between dependent, developmentally immature children in the same family constitutes sibling incest. Most often, it is kept secret. Such incest can range from inappropriate touching or fondling to sexual kissing and hugging to intercourse. Less obvious forms include staring at a sister or brother in a sexual way, ridiculing a sibling's body parts, taking or showing pornographic photographs, or reading sexually explicit material aloud.

Victims of sibling incest are typically between 5 and 11 years of age, with the perpetrator being anywhere from 3 to 11 years older. A survey of 796 New England college undergraduates conducted by David Finkelhor found that 40 percent of the respondents who reported sibling incest were less than 8 years old at the time of the abuse. But sexual relationships between siblings can occur at any age.

The type of incestuous activity varies by age. Younger children are more likely to engage in genital exhibition, whereas older ones are more likely to perform, or at least attempt, intercourse. In some cases an act of sibling incest happens only once, while in other cases the acts occur repeatedly. Although cases of sibling sexual relationships continuing for as long as 12 years have been reported, most go on for less than a year.

How prevalent is sibling incest? Current estimates are probably too low, because many studies are too small to apply across the entire population—and many of the siblings involved don't want to admit their behavior. Finkelhor's research at a New England college offers some insight. In this study, 15 percent of the females and 10 percent of the males reported having experienced sibling sexual activity. Of these, 74 percent reported heterosexual experiences. Of the other 26 percent, 16 percent of the incest cases were between brothers and 10 percent were between sisters. One overall estimate puts the rate of brother-sister incest at about five times the rate of parent-child incest. However, more studies are needed to give a truly accurate estimation.

THE EFFECTS OF SIBLING INCEST

Traditionally, the common view has been that incest between an adult and a child is more traumatic than sexual contact between siblings. But with more studies being conducted and more personal accounts gathered, that perception is beginning to change. Regardless of who the perpetrator is, incest can seriously damage the victim.

EMOTIONAL IMPACT

The short- and long-term problems suffered by children and teens who have been sexually abused by a sibling can include low self-esteem. They can also involve guilt and depression. Because the victims feel betrayed by someone so close to them, many find it difficult to trust again and fear they would be vulnerable in any intimate relationship.

In most studies, sisters have been the victims of sexual abuse by their brothers. Not surprisingly, they have experienced more long-term effects than have their perpetrating brothers. Marie's story is a good example.

> My older brother started to touch me sexually when I was 8 and he was 13. At first, I liked all the attention and the treats he brought me. As the abuse went on, I wanted him to stop, but he wouldn't. He threatened to tell our parents I'd done something bad if I told about the abuse. I thought they'd believe him. He finally left home when he was 19 and the abuse stopped. I was 14.

> When he was gone I thought that was the end of feeling bad. But it wasn't. Everyone I dated treated me like I didn't matter. I kept trying to get them to love me even when I didn't like them.

In Marie's case, her brother was nice to her in the beginning, bribing her with treats and the promise of special attention. As the incestuous relationship continued, however, she became confused. She began to believe that he—or anyone—would love her only if she did what that person wanted. She presumed that sex was the price she'd have to pay for attention and that her feelings and needs weren't important.

Some incest victims suffer anxiety attacks, sleep disturbances, or symptoms of post-traumatic stress disorder—amnesia, nightmares, and flashbacks. If they isolate themselves from social groups, they may be perceived as loners by others. Some individuals resort to alcohol and drug abuse or, worse, attempt suicide. In addition to the emotional and

For years afterward, incest victims can suffer anxiety attacks, nightmares, flashbacks, and many other disturbing psychological symptoms, including problems in their own sexual development.

psychological effects, physical injury is the result of some sibling incest cases.

IMPACT ON SEXUAL DEVELOPMENT

Sibling incest can have a long-term negative impact on sexual development. According to researchers like Pam Ramsey, if a girl's first sexual experience is with an older brother in a coercive, secretive, guilt-ridden atmosphere, her sense of sexual identity can become warped. Her guilt and shame can become identified with her sexuality, thus producing sexual dysfunction that ranges from pain during intercourse to anxiety attacks to abstaining from sex altogether.

Many victims react by becoming sexually promiscuous, confusing intimacy with sexuality. They may find it difficult to trust men in general, or they may use sex as the only way to relate to men. Some may grow up feeling unworthy of supportive relationships and never go on to marry.

The incestuous experience makes women feel more vulnerable. For instance, they're likely to be more upset by men's sexual comments or advances, by being asked to pose for erotic pictures, or by a "peeping Tom" or exhibitionist. According to D. E. H. Russell in *The Secret Trauma*, these women also tend to be more afraid of sexual assault as adults than do women who have never been incestuously abused.

These fears are not groundless. A woman who has experienced brother-sister incest appears to be a more likely target of later victimization than does a woman who has never been the victim of incest. Russell's research suggests that such a woman may marry a man who becomes physically violent toward her. Or she may succumb to unwanted sexual interaction with an authority figure or with a girl or another woman.

CATEGORIES OF SIBLING INCEST

Incestuous abuse can range in severity from unforced (yet unwanted) kissing to forcible rape. Some researchers have divided sibling incest into two basic types. One is less abusive, and it may have something of a nurturing motive. The other is exploitative, coercive, and often violent. In this second type, power and dominance are the motives, and psychological and emotional damage are the likely consequences.

Most cases of brother-sister incest do not involve mutual desire, and they are often destructive. The greater the degree of force used, the more destructive the impact. Also, the younger the abused child and the longer the period of abuse, the worse the likely consequences will be. Russell found that in 44 percent of brother-sister incest cases the brothers used force, compared with 25 percent of all other cases of incest. In Finkelhor's study, 64 percent of the students who reported that force was used described the experience as negative. And the greater the age difference between siblings, the more likely it was that the experience was negative.

Clearly, then, coercive sibling incest has painful consequences. But what about the other variety of sibling incest? If the behavior is of the less abusive type, can it possibly be harmless, or even in some ways positive? According to C. Loredo, some sibling incest can arise out of a set of needs that both children have, such as "a desire for affiliation and affection; a combating of loneliness, depression, and a sense of isolation; and a discharging of anxiety and tension due to stress." Or a younger sister may initially agree to take part in her brother's desire to fool around, though she doesn't fully understand what that means.

There are also notions that some brother-sister incest can positively affect one's sexual self-image later in life—if the experience grows out of the natural curiosity or need for experimentation of young children, and if children are not traumatized by disapproving adults who discover their activity. But this argument may apply only to the traditional "playing doctor" games of very young, same-aged children—games that, strictly speaking, do not meet our definition of incest.

It is important to remember that cases of sexual contact between brothers and sisters that *appear* to be mutually desired usually are not—and the effects can be just as damaging as with forced incest. According to Ramsey's 1994 report, even in cases in which both siblings initially felt positive or ambivalent about the incestuous behavior, most eventually felt shame—with the sister tending to experience great remorse and trauma. And most professionals acknowledge that they have never seen a female patient who considered incest to be anything but a negative experience.

Unfortunately, the research to date is incomplete, because the majority of those involved in sibling sexual experience—especially those who have sex with a much older sibling—don't tell anyone about it. As Michael Kahn and Genevieve Monks note, this fact in itself implies that the participants feel shame or guilt and are suffering emotionally.

WHAT CAUSES SIBLING INCEST?

Research has shown that in healthy, nurturing family environments, children develop secure bonds with their parents and siblings at a young age. When there is a strong familial bond, incest is much less likely to occur. With the increased incidence of divorce and remarriage, such a bond is often missing in families.

DISRUPTED FAMILY ENVIRONMENTS

In family environments that have been disrupted in some way, there are several possible contributors to the emergence of incest. These include:

- If a parent who was sexually or physically abused as a child then molests or beats his or her children, the cycle of abuse is likely to be continued between the siblings.

In a family with strong, secure bonds between parents and children, sibling incest is less likely to occur than in a disrupted family.

- Brother-sister incest tends to occur in families in which parents provide poor supervision. For example, giving an older brother too much responsibility in taking care of his younger siblings can lead to a variety of abuses.
- Sibling incest often occurs in homes in which the parents permit seductive behavior or engage in such behavior themselves.

■　　　■　　　■

The case of a young man named Dave, reported by Canada's National Clearinghouse on Family Violence, illustrates how multiple factors can interact and culminate in sibling incest. Dave, who was 15 years old, was

Responsibility is often good for children. Sometimes, though, when a brother has to spend a great deal of time caring for younger children, the situation may become an invitation to abuse.

dared by some of his classmates to have sex with a girl. Afraid to even talk to a girl, let alone ask one for a date, Dave was intimidated by his more sexually active peers. One night, while baby-sitting his younger sister Sharon, he forced her to have sexual intercourse.

Fortunately, Sharon told her mother, who in turn sought help. The mother told the counselor that on a number of occasions the children's father had forced sex on her in front of them. She also admitted that her husband often beat her if she didn't prepare his meals on time. Clearly, Dave had learned from his father that it was all right for a male family member to use force—in sex and other matters—on a female in the family.

■   ■   ■

Ramsey, in her 1994 report, pointed out that some families show another dynamic. A sexually repressive atmosphere in the home may have the same ultimate effect as the too-open sexual behavior in Dave's home—that is, it may increase the children's interest in the forbidden. Moreover, when parents are distant and neglectful, rejecting and discouraging, or incapable of open communication, siblings may turn to each other for comfort and contact. In such a setting, older siblings may pressure or manipulate younger ones into a sexual relationship.

OTHER FAMILY FACTORS

Evidence also shows that large family size increases the risk of sibling incest. Besides pointing to problems of parental supervision, this link suggests that poverty and poor physical and psychological boundaries play a role. In *The Secret Trauma*, Russell reports that 77 percent of the female victims of sibling incest—a figure more than double that of incest victims in general—came from families with six or more members. Only 5 percent of these victims were aware that their brothers were sexually abusing another relative, which indicates that secrecy was critical to the incidents.

Secrecy, in fact, is a weapon in most incest cases. An older brother may convince his younger sister to keep their relationship a secret through intimidation, threats, bribes, or the offer of special attention. Because the victim probably experiences guilt and shame, she may already feel that she has to remain silent about what happened. Worse, she may come to believe that she was to blame for what was done to her, especially if she experienced physical pleasure during the abuse. Also, she may find it hard to admit what happened for fear of destroying the family. Such fear only reinforces the secrecy of the abuse, causing even more psychological stress for the victim. The fact that incest is so often hidden from others also makes it more likely to recur.

THE ROLE OF SOCIETY

Many observers contend that social conditioning is partly to blame for the disproportionate number of female victims of incest. Because our society encourages males to be self-reliant and females not to exercise power but to nurture others at their own expense, a sister, regardless of age difference, may find it difficult to refuse sexual contact with a brother. Thus, males have a clear advantage, from both the power given them by society and sheer physical size. As Ramsey puts it, if a sister feels powerless or threatened, whether influenced by social pressures or by the hierarchy in her own family, she might submit as a means of "survival."

Power relates to age differences as well as gender. Traditionally, sibling incest has not been given the same attention as parent-child incest, in part because we believe that a mother or father wields much more power over a child than does a brother or sister. However, as Kahn and Monks report, mental health professionals have found that children and adolescents can perceive someone only seven years older than themselves to have significant authority them. This suggests that in a family an older sibling often has significantly more power than a younger one—at least in the younger one's mind.

In addition to social aspects of power, social stigmas play a significant role. The shame and guilt attached to incest encourage the victims as well as the abusers to keep the matter secret, and this enables the incestuous relationship to continue unchecked in too many cases. In the past two decades, parent-child incest has been openly confronted more than ever before, but the public still does not want to acknowledge sexual relations between brothers and sisters. The subject remains taboo. Certainly, sibling incest is not a pleasant topic, but it does occur. And the victims suffer all the more because of the lack of support from family and society, which tend to blame them for the abuse.

In contrast to the tendency to stigmatize, sexual acts by teens are often dismissed or minimized as being just experimentation or harmless curiosity. Some may feel that incest, in particular, is a matter to be dealt with by the family. Unfortunately, as D. T. Marsh points out,

WARNING SIGNS FOR SIBLING ABUSE

The following list of symptoms was compiled by the Sibling Abuse Survivors' Information and Advocacy Network, located in Sebring, Florida (see Appendix: For More Information). Any such warning sign may indicate another type of problem, but many victims of sibling abuse show one or more of these symptoms.

- Failure to thrive
- Weight loss or gain
- Anxiety and/or depression
- Listlessness
- Phobias or irrational/inexplicable fears
- Issues of personal space or privacy
- Difficulty with authority

- Difficulty sleeping; insomnia; fear of the dark
- Passivity
- Low self-esteem
- Nightmares
- Anger
- Emotional outbursts
- Frequent illness
- Withdrawal

Depression, listlessness, and withdrawal are among the warning signs for sibling abuse.

offenders rarely seek treatment on their own, and left unchallenged they may broaden their target range.

In 1986 Becker and colleagues published a study of adolescents charged with sibling incest. The researchers found that these young people had actually committed more sexual crimes than they had been charged with. Of the 22 subjects studied, nearly half reported that they had engaged in other, nonincestuous sex with minors. But nearly one-third denied all deviant sexual behavior—in other words, they didn't believe that having sex with a brother or sister was wrong.

What does this mean for society? Although it is not inevitable, a number of those who commit sexual assault within the family may go on to commit sexual crimes against the general public. This is all the more reason for society to recognize the existence of sibling incest, attempt to prevent it, and provide treatment for the youngsters involved.

TREATMENT OPTIONS

As with most painful experiences, the sooner people get help, the better off they will be. In the case of sibling incest, at least two people need help—the victim and the abuser.

TREATMENT FOR THE VICTIM

For a victim of sibling incest, the recovery process begins when she admits she was abused and recognizes that she can't handle the situation on her own. Services and resources are available for incest victims, whether they seek help as children, adolescents, or adults. But even professional treatment may involve a number of difficulties, as Pam Ramsey's story of a young woman named Pat demonstrates:

> Pat, who is now 27 years old, was sexually abused by her older brother. She's not certain exactly how old she was when the abuse first occurred, but believes it happened the summer between 8th and 9th grades when she was 14 and her brother was 17. She is the only daughter in the family.
>
> Pat remembers herself as a happy, normal, active teenager, although very shy around boys. When she was 18 (after the abuse had stopped), her mother placed her in therapy to uncover why her daughter had gained so much weight. Pat knew why, but she couldn't share it with the therapist or anyone. She had been a nor-

Because of the difference in their ages, this eight-year-old boy would perceive his 16-year-old brother as having a great deal of authority.

mal-sized child before the abuse, but rapidly became obese during her high school years and even more so while in college. After several sessions of doing nothing but cry, Pat stopped going to therapy.

She had always remembered the abuse but only started to truly confront her painful memories when she entered group counseling. She is still very ashamed about the incidences with her brother. Although she intellectually knows it wasn't her fault, emotionally she isn't sure. A couple of years ago, when she was 25, she told her mother what had happened. Now, she feels the added guilt of having changed her mother's relationship with her brother. And she is obsessed with trying to figure out why, as a child, she allowed her brother to do what he did to her.

Pat has had no sexual contact with any males since the abuse occurred. She doesn't even date, although she is obsessed with sexual thoughts and is prone to severe depression.

Even though a decade has passed since Pat's brother last sexually abused her, Pat still carries the emotional scars of incest. Whether an incest victim endures an isolated incident of abuse or ongoing assaults over an extended period, the process of recovery can be exceptionally painful and difficult.

■   ■   ■

Many communities have support groups for teenage girls who have been sexually abused. Typically, a counselor will help them make the group a safe place to discuss their victimization and how it has affected the way they feel about other areas of their lives—parents, school, friends, boyfriends, sex, drugs. Members of the group may also practice role-playing to learn how to deal with intimidating situations, such as male sexual advances. Since many adolescents who have endured incest feel different from other teenagers, the support group initially may be the only place they are comfortable.

Support groups and other forms of counseling may incorporate art therapy as a way to work through the painful memories. For example, some victims might draw pictures of their nightmares or of the abuse itself as a way of bringing it out in the open. Others may vent their emotions by making a clay sculpture of their abuser and then smashing it.

For an incest victim, the first step in getting help is to tell someone, such as a good friend.

In addition to seeking out support groups, the victim of incest may require individual therapy to help her understand that she is not to blame. Remember Marie, whose story appeared earlier in this chapter? She describes her process of recovery this way:

> One day, I told my best friend about my brother. She told her mom, who reported the abuse. My parents were upset when they found out, but now I'm glad they know. A counselor helped me understand that the abuse wasn't my fault. She helped me see I deserve to be treated with respect.

In contrast to Pat, Marie reached out to a friend, whose support led her to professional counseling early on. By not keeping her abuse a secret, Marie began to move beyond the incest to deal openly with her fears and insecurities.

TREATMENT FOR THE OFFENDER

What about the perpetrator of incest? The abusive brother or sister—and often the whole family—can also benefit from therapy. In fact, counseling for both the abuser and the victim is usually necessary for their relationship to heal and move beyond the incest.

The odds of a sexual offender's seeking treatment are small, but it does happen. If the victim or someone else reports the abuse—to the police, hospital, child services agency, or other family welfare service—the abuser will probably face criminal charges. Adolescent offenders like Dave may be put on probation. Although the court may allow them to live at home, they will likely be forced to get counseling for sibling sexual offenders. In Dave's case, in fact, both he and his sister started sexual abuse therapy and moved into a transition house while their mother decided whether or not to stay with their father.

In Dave's counseling sessions, he learned social skills to help him get along better with other teenagers, and he discovered how to control the abusive behavior he had copied from his father. He also learned to take responsibility for his actions. (Dave's father was also charged by the court to seek counseling and to change the way he treated women and children.)

If offenses are serious enough, a teenage abuser can be confined for some period in a detention center. There, treatment may mean attending group sessions in which the offenders confront their behavior. Then individual therapy can help each one understand why he acted as he did. Basic social skills, such as how to ask for a date, may also be taught, along with appropriate sexual behavior. Most important, such counseling can help prevent the adolescent offender from growing into an adult offender.

The death of a young brother or sister can affect a child for a long time afterward.

6

DEATH OF A SIBLING

Young people aren't supposed to die. They are supposed to live long, happy lives. When a child or teenager dies, the entire family is thrown into a state of shock. "How can this happen—he was so young?" is the often-unanswerable question family members ask themselves. When it's a brother or sister who dies, part of the surviving sibling's identity perishes as well.

The effects of a sibling's death vary, depending on the surviving child's relationship with the deceased child. For most brothers and sisters, the loss of a sibling means, at the very least, the loss of a playmate and close companion. A young boy may have lost an older brother who had always been his protector. The death of a baby may bring on great despair in an older sister who derived great satisfaction from mothering the infant. Although children can recover from the loss, the experience will affect them long after the sibling is buried.

Anger in response to the death of a loved one is a universal reaction, seen in both children and adults. Its eruption after the death of a sibling is illustrated by a passage from J. D. Salinger's famous novel *The Catcher in the Rye:*

> My brother Allie . . . got leukemia and died when we were up in Maine. . . . I slept in the garage the night he died, and I broke all the goddam windows with my fist, just for the hell of it. . . . It was a very stupid thing to do, I'll admit, but I hardly didn't even know I was doing it, and you didn't know Allie.

This response, to give it a simple name, is aggression. According to research summarized by Lindsey Kiefner and coauthors, more than half of those aged 4 to 16 who lose a sibling show highly inflated aggression scores on the *Child Behavior Checklist,* a commonly used behavioral test. Children and adolescents tend to carry out their aggression through hostility toward peers and family members and through blatant physical violence. And they become aggressive not only to vent their internal anger and hostility, but also to gain the attention of their parents, who are absorbed with their own grief.

Children who have lost a sister or brother may also react with a number of other emotions, including guilt, confusion, depression, and loneliness. Their thoughts and feelings may be in such turmoil that they change from one moment to the next. Guilt, a common emotion, may stem simply from being alive when the sibling is dead or from having been well when the sibling was ill. Or it may come from having wished the sibling dead, or at least having wished that the brother or sister would not get so much attention.

How do these feelings show themselves? At school, youngsters may become distracted or disruptive, causing their friendships as well as their academic work to suffer. They may withdraw socially and develop an increased dependence on their parents. Difficulty sleeping, hallucinations about their dead sibling, fear of death, and thoughts of suicide are also not unusual.

As for longer-term effects, the child's age at the time of the sibling's death is a key predictor. J. H. Fanos and B. J. Nickerson identified the ages of 13 to 17 as the time during which sibling deaths have the most profound effects on the survivors. Persons who lose a brother or sister during these years show not only the common anxiety and survivor's guilt, but also greater bodily concerns and fear of intimacy well into late adolescence and adulthood.

As Kiefner and coauthors explain, a study of adolescents under 19 years of age who have lost a sibling showed that, seven to nine years after the sibling's death, this group had significantly more anxiety, depression, and guilt than did their peers. In general, most of us require only about two years to deal with the death of a loved one.

Thus, it appears that adolescence is the most emotionally devastating time to lose a sibling. Perhaps this is because adolescents have had years to develop a strong emotional bond with their siblings, yet they haven't fully developed the independence of adulthood. The teenage years are an emotional period even in a stable family environment, and the turmoil of losing a sibling will only add to the turbulence of this stage of life.

FACTORS THAT SLOW A SIBLING'S RECOVERY

The circumstances surrounding the death of a sibling—sudden versus anticipated death, supportive versus self-absorbed parents—con-

Adolescents who have lost a sibling often feel more depressed and guilty than their peers.

tribute greatly to the time it takes survivors to get over the loss. For example, if a brother commits suicide and his sister discovers the body, she is likely to be much more devastated than if he had died after a long bout with cancer. However, death after an extended illness is also quite traumatic. Obviously, too, the closer the siblings have been, the greater the sense of loss and separation after a death.

Parents who are wrapped up in their own grief may react to a sibling's mourning with silence or irritation, which may cause the child to feel he or she is being blamed for the death. This reaction by the parents also helps teach the child to deny feelings, thus inhibiting the mourning process necessary for healing. H. Rosen's 1986 study of adults who had lost a sibling during childhood found that three-quarters of the participants had not spoken to *anyone* about their feelings. Some simply had no one to turn to at the time of the death; others had suppressed their own feelings of loss in order to spare their parents any more pain. Unfortunately, well-meaning friends and relatives may contribute to this stoic behavior by encouraging the surviving children to "be strong" and put their parents' needs before their own.

On the other hand, some siblings are stifled in their attempts at recovery because their parents become overprotective. For instance, as Michael Kahn and Genevieve Monks report, parents who have lost a baby may overly coddle the surviving sister or brother, often causing the child to struggle with two identities and feel burdened or guilty. Later, especially during adolescence, the sibling may take death-defying risks to prove that he or she is invulnerable to the fate of the deceased sibling.

THE ROLE OF SOCIETY

We live in a culture that does very little to help us come to terms with death—especially that of a brother or sister. Our society doesn't educate us to deal with loss, but rather teaches us how to acquire and hold on to things. Because of this, we are ill-prepared to handle death.

Some say that we are better prepared to deal with minor accidents than with death and emotional loss, because in our world they get more attention. Think about it: Classes are offered in simple first aid and in health and safety, both by schools and by local Red Cross chapters. We all know to dial 911 in case of an emergency. But when is the last time you took a class on death and dying? There is no 911 for mourning, although certain organizations have established toll-free hotlines that are open on a limited basis (see Appendix: For More Information). As J. W. James and F. Cherry explain in *The Grief Recovery Handbook,* this is a serious issue in our society. Each year, deaths leave behind approximately eight million new grievers.

TREATMENT OPTIONS

There are many ways in which brothers and sisters can be helped through the mourning process. If the death comes after a long struggle with disease, the surviving children will feel a much greater sense of security if their parents were regularly available to them during the sibling's illness. After the death, as Buz and Joanie Overbeck point out, siblings benefit from parents who encourage grieving and openness by sharing their own grief and expressing their feelings in front of their children. In any case, grieving that includes talking about the qualities of the child who died (both positive and negative ones), as well as the differences between the siblings (both good and bad) can help the survivors put the death in perspective.

Talking with parents about death can help surviving siblings cope with grief and loss.

A sibling's reaction to a death and the time it takes him or her to recover can also be greatly improved if parents explain death itself, and the process of dying, clearly and adequately. It is especially important that they focus some discussion on the surviving sibling's sense of loss.

In general, as Kahn and Monks suggest, families that communicate

HOW A SURVIVING SIBLING FEELS

I n *Helping Children Cope with Loss,* Buz and Joanie Overbeck mention a number of feelings that are normal—not unusual—for a child whose sibling has died. These include:

- Impatience and anger at the world
- Resentment about the attention the parents are getting
- Resentment about the attention the surviving child is *not* getting
- Resentment about having to do more around the home

Strong doses of parental attention and affection can reduce a surviving sibling's guilt, resentment, and fears.

- Fear of having to "replace" the sibling somehow
- Guilt about feeling relief at the death after a long illness
- Guilt about "bad" thoughts, nasty words, and fights with the deceased

Again, these are normal reactions, and with the support of parents, relatives, and friends, most children will cope with them. They do not mean the sister or brother has an unusual problem. If such feelings become extremely intense, however, or if they persist for a long while in a strong form, the child may need some special help.

openly or have a strong religious faith tend to fare much better in the long run. When a family is tightly knit and encourages intellectual or cultural activity, active recreation, and social involvement, siblings are more apt to come to terms with their grief in a shorter period of time.

CONCERNS FOR TEENAGERS

A number of writers and researchers have focused especially on the reactions of teenagers to a sibling's death. In *Straight Talk About Death for Teenagers*, E. A. Grollman quotes a surviving adolescent: "Everyone's trying to help the little kids or parents, but what about us? Don't we count?" This is often the way adolescents feel when a brother or sister has died.

Those around a surviving teenager may erroneously think that the parents hurt the most and that the younger children in the family need protecting. Relatives and family friends may assume that older siblings don't need special support. But teens do need comfort, says Grollman. They may feel emotionally dazed or deeply depressed. They may experience a sense of disbelief about the sibling's death. Whatever their feelings may be, they need to discuss them with others who are supportive. A pain that is buried becomes a time bomb waiting to explode.

James and Cherry point out that adolescents need to understand that getting over the death of a sibling doesn't mean forgetting or never missing the deceased. They should be able to enjoy fond memories without guilt, regret, or remorse. They should understand that it's all right to feel bad from time to time and to talk about those feelings.

Friends are a vital source of support for teens who have lost a brother or sister.

SUPPORT GROUPS AND THERAPY

Although it is often enough to work through the loss of a brother or sister with family members, some surviving siblings may feel the need to discuss their feelings with peers. For them, support groups are available, many of which are sponsored by local schools, churches, synagogues, funeral homes, hospitals, or community groups. National organizations such as the Dougy Center, which offers the National Directory of Children's Grief Support Systems, can help families locate agencies that provide assistance (see Appendix: For More Information).

Members of teen support groups can share concerns and fears with others their own age who have been through similar experiences. They may cry, open up, eventually even laugh—all of which helps them to lessen the loneliness they feel. As Grollman says, one of the best outcomes of support groups is that newcomers gain hope and encouragement when they see that others have survived their own losses.

For those who need more intense therapy, grief counseling comes in many forms. Those who have strong religious faith may get the help they need from a minister, priest, rabbi, or other member of the clergy. Other survivors may turn to a counselor or grief therapist, by themselves or with other family members.

Individual psychotherapy may be necessary for more severe cases. Grollman argues that if a surviving sibling has very intense symptoms—being unable to sleep, becoming persistently indifferent to school and life, constantly erupting in anger, or considering suicide—professional treatment may be warranted.

Good sibling relationships have a strong positive effect on a child's development.

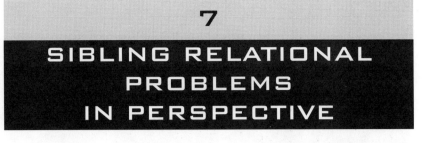

7

SIBLING RELATIONAL PROBLEMS IN PERSPECTIVE

Despite the topic of this volume, our relationships with our brothers and sisters generally have a positive influence on our lives. The ways we interact with our siblings greatly contribute to our psychological, emotional, and social development.

Interestingly, studies conducted in the past two decades have indicated that even birth order—where we fall in the family line—has a great deal to do with how we communicate with others. Our interaction with our brothers and sisters, after all, is one of our earliest instances of social interaction. Indeed, healthy relationships between siblings can help build a solid personal foundation from which we derive great strength and security throughout life.

Dysfunctional sibling relationships, on the other hand, can shake a person's confidence and lead to serious difficulties later on. Some harmful behavior, like aggression or incest, may be handed down from generation to generation. Other problems, like the death or disability of a brother or sister, are quite frequently a surprise, and they challenge families with additional hurdles.

In reality, sibling relational problems do not result from one particular cause. They come about because a variety of factors work together to enhance or aggravate family relationships. Exceptional family conflict, crisis, or change is the usual suspect. For example, the death of one family member is the type of crisis that strains a family's emotional stability—at least for some time. Similarly, the breakup of a family by divorce can disrupt the lives of children.

Despite the many differences among the sibling relational problems discussed in this book, they all share a common principle: The sooner these diffi-

Our brothers and sisters give us some of our earliest lessons in social interaction.

culties are confronted, the better off those involved will be. There is no medication or therapy that can replace reaching out to family members and supportive friends. Children and adolescents who have a strong support system—including parents, other relatives, friends, and community or religious groups—are the most likely to overcome sibling relational problems and live healthy and productive lives.

APPENDIX

FOR MORE INFORMATION

Many social service agencies and nonprofit organizations offer literature, support, and other services for children and adolescents who need help breaking free of an incestuous relationship, overcoming the death of a sibling, or handling other problems related to family relationships. Many of the national groups also have state and local chapters and World Wide Web sites.

GENERAL

National Coalition Against Domestic Violence
P.O. Box 34103
Washington, DC 20043-4103
(202) 638-6388
TTY (202) 737-3033

The National Committee to Prevent Child Abuse (NCPCA)
332 South Michigan Ave.
Suite 1600
Chicago, IL 60604
(800) CHILDREN, (312) 663-3520
Publications: (800) 55-NCPCA

National Council on Child Abuse and Family Violence
1155 Connecticut Ave., NW
Suite 400
Washington, DC 20036
(800) 222-2000, (202) 429-6695

National Network for Youth
1319 F St., NW
Suite 401
Washington, DC 20004
(202) 783-7949

MENTAL AND PHYSICAL ILLNESS

Alberta Committee of Citizens with Disabilities (ACCD)
In Canada: (800) 387-2514
http://indie.ca/accd/

The Arc
National Headquarters
P.O. Box 1047
Arlington, TX 76004
(817) 261-6003
TDD (817) 277-0553
E-mail: thearc@metronet.com

Band-Aides and Blackboards
http://funrsc.fairfield.edu/~jfleitas/
contents.html

Canadian Mental Health Association (CMHA)
970 Lawrence Ave. West
Suite 205
Toronto, Ontario M6A 3B6
Canada
(416) 789-7957

National Alliance for the Mentally Ill Child and Adolescent Network (NAMI-CAN)
200 North Glebe Rd.
Suite 1015
Arlington, VA 22203-3754
(800) 950-NAMI

Sibling Information Network
The A. J. Pappanikou Center
991 Main St.
East Hartford, CT 06108
(860) 282-7050

Sibling Support Project
Children's Hospital and Medical Center
4800 Sand Point Way NE
Seattle, WA 98105
(206) 368-4911

SibNet
http://www.chmc.org/departmt/ sib-
supp

INCEST

C. Henry Kempe National Center for Prevention and Treatment of Child Abuse and Neglect
1205 Oneida St.
Denver, CO 80220
(303) 321-3963

Childhelp USA
IOF Foresters National Child Abuse
Hotline
(800) 422-4453 (4-A-CHILD)

Family Violence and Sexual Assault Institute
1121 East Southeast Loop 323
Suite 130
Tyler, TX 75701
(903) 534-5100

Incest Resources, Inc.
Cambridge Women's Center
46 Pleasant St.
Cambridge, MA 02139
(617) 354-8807

Incest Survivors Resource Network International
P.O. Box 7375
Las Cruces, NM 88006-7375
(505) 521-4260

Sibling Abuse Survivors' Information and Advocacy Network
P.O. Box 301
Sebring, FL 33871-0301
http://www.sasian.org/

Survivors of Incest Anonymous
World Service Office
P.O. Box 21817
Baltimore, MD 21222-6817
(410) 282-3400

VOICES in Action, Inc.
(Victims of Incest Can Emerge
Survivors)
P.O. Box 148309
Chicago, IL 60614
(312) 327-1500, (800) 7-VOICE-8
http://www.voices-action.org

DEATH

The Dougy Center
The National Center for Grieving
Children and Families
P. O. Box 86852
Portland, OR 97286
(503) 775-5683
Fax: (503) 777-3097
http://www.dougy.org

Fernside
2303 Indian Mound Ave.
Cincinnati, OH 45212
(513) 841-1012
Fax: (513) 841-1546

The Grief Recovery Institute
8306 Wilshire Blvd., #21-A
Los Angeles, CA 90211
(800) 445-4808

APPENDIX

DIAGNOSTIC CRITERIA

Because problems in sibling relations come in such a large variety, the diagnostic criteria are somewhat generalized. The following passages from the Diagnostic and Statistical Manual of Mental Disorders *define first* relational problems *and then, in that context, the category known as* sibling relational problem. *Notice the emphasis on impaired functioning and on consideration of the entire family or "relational unit."*

Relational Problems

Relational problems include patterns of interaction between or among members of a relational unit that are associated with clinically significant impairment in functioning, or symptoms among one or more members of the relational unit, or impairment in the functioning of the relational unit itself. . . . These problems may exacerbate or complicate the management of a mental disorder or general medical condition in one or more members of the relational unit, may be a result of a mental disorder or a general medical condition, may be independent of other conditions that are present, or can occur in the absence of any other condition.

V61.8 Sibling Relational Problem

This category should be used when the focus of clinical attention is a pattern of interaction among siblings that is associated with clinically significant impairment in individual or family functioning or the development of symptoms in one or more of the siblings.

APPENDIX

BIBLIOGRAPHY

Azmitia, M., and J. Hesser. "Why Siblings Are Important Agents of Cognitive Development: A Comparison of Siblings and Peers." *Child Development* 64 (1993): 430–444.

Bard, M. "The Study and Modification of Intra-family Violence." In *The Control of Aggression and Violence,* edited by J. L. Singer, 149–163. New York: Academic Press, 1971.

Bass, E., and L. Davis. *The Courage to Heal: A Guide for Women Survivors of Child Sexual Abuse.* 3d ed. New York: HarperCollins, 1994.

Becker, J. V., et al. "Characteristics of Adolescent Incest Sexual Perpetrators: Preliminary Findings. *Journal of Family Violence* 1 (1986): 85–97.

Booth, W. "Hidden Specter of Sibling Abuse." *Washington Post,* 14 August 1998, A3.

Caruso, B. *The Impact of Incest.* Center City, Minn.: Hazelden Educational Materials, 1987.

Crittenden, P. "Sibling Interaction: Evidence of a Generational Effect in Maltreating Infants." *Child Abuse and Neglect* 8 (1984).

Doidge, N., et al. "Characteristics of Psychoanalytic Patients Under a Nationalized Health Plan: DSM-III-R Diagnoses, Previous Treatment, and Childhood Trauma." *American Journal of Psychiatry* 151, no 4 (April 1994).

Erickson, M. T. "Rethinking Oedipus: An Evolutionary Perspective of Incest Avoidance." *American Journal of Psychiatry* 150, no 3 (March 1993).

Fanos, J. H., and B. G. Nickerson. "Long-Term Effects of Sibling Death During Adolescence." *Journal of Adolescent Research* 6: 70–82.

Felson, R. B., and N. Russo. "Parental Punishment and Sibling Aggression." *Social Psychology Quarterly* 51 (1988).

Finkelhor, D. "Sex Among Siblings: A Survey on Prevalence, Variety, and Effects." *Archives of Sexual Behavior* 9, no 3 (June 1980): 171–194.

Fisman, S., et al. "Risk and Protective Factors Affecting the Adjustment of Siblings of Children with Chronic Disabilities." *Journal of American Academy of Child and Adolescent Psychiatry* 35, no 11 (November 1996).

Freud, S. "The Aetiology of Hysteria" (1896). In *The Standard Edition of the Complete Psychological Works of Sigmund Freud.* Edited and translated by J. Strachey. Vol. 3. London: Hogarth Press, 1962–1964.

Gath, A. "Sibling Reactions to Mental Handicap: A Comparison of the Brothers and Sisters of Mongol Children." *Journal of Child Psychology and Psychiatry and Allied Disciplines* 15 (1974).

Green, A. H. "Victims of Child Abuse." *Review of Psychiatry* 13, sec. 4 (1994).

Grollman, E. A. *Straight Talk About Death for Teenagers: How to Cope with Losing Someone You Love.* Boston: Beacon Press, 1993.

Gully, K. J., et al. "Research Note: Sibling Contribution to Violent Behavior." *Journal of Marriage and the Family* 43 (1981).

Howe, N. "Sibling-Directed Internal State Language, Perspective Taking, and Affective Behavior." *Child Development* 62 (1991): 1503–1512.

Itzkowitz, J. "Fostering Supportive Relationships: Remember the Siblings." *Springboard* 1, no. 2 (Fall 1991).

James, J. W., and F. Cherry. *The Grief Recovery Handbook: A Step-by-Step Program for Moving Beyond Loss.* New York: Harper and Row, 1989.

Kahn, M. D., and G. Monks. "Sibling Relational Problems." *DSM-IV Sourcebook,* vol 3. Washington, D.C.: American Psychiatric Press, 1997.

Kiefner, L., G. Buckley, and L. Madonia. "Sibling Relationships." 1998. Available at http:// www.student.richmond.edu/~lmadonia/sibling.html.

Koch, H. L. "The Relation of Certain Formal Attributes of Siblings to Attitudes Held Toward Each Other and Toward Their Parents." *Monographs of the Society for Research in Child Development* 24, no. 4 (serial no. 78) (1960).

Lavigne, J. V., and M. Ryan. "Psychologic Adjustment of Siblings of Children with Chronic Illness." *Pediatrics* 63 (1979).

Loredo, C. "Sibling Incest." In *Handbook of Clinical Intervention in Child Sexual Abuse,* 177–189. Lexington, Mass: D. C. Heath, 1982.

Marsh, D. T. "Siblings: Forgotten Family Members." *Journal of the California Alliance for the Mentally Ill* 3, no. 1. Available at: http:// www. mhsource. com/hy/j31.html.

————, R. M. Dickens, and E. F. Torrey. *How to Cope with Mental Illness in Your Family: A Self-Care Guide for Siblings, Offspring, and Parents.* New York: Putnam, 1997.

Meyer, D., and P. Vadasy. *Living with a Brother or Sister with Special Needs: A Book for Sibs.* 2d ed. Seattle: University of Washington Press, 1996. Available at: http://www.chmc.org/departmt/sibsupp/.

Minnett, A. M., D. L. Vandell, and J. W. Santrock. "The Effects of Sibling Status on Sibling Interaction: Influence of Birth Order, Age, Spacing, Sex of Child, and Sex of Sibling." *Child Development* 54 (1983).

National Center for Victims of Crime. "Infolink: Incest." 1997. Available at: http://www.nvc.org/infolink/info29.html/.

National Clearinghouse on Family Violence. *Sibling Sexual Abuse.* Sexual Abuse Information Series II. Ottawa: Health Canada, 1994.

————. *When Teenage Girls Have Been Sexually Abused: A Guide for Teenagers.* Sexual Abuse Information Series II. Ottawa: Health Canada, 1994.

Overbeck, B., and J. Overbeck. *Helping Children Cope with Loss.* Dallas: TLC Group, 1995.

Ramsey, P. "Psychological Effects of Incest on Girls, Focusing on Sibling Incest." 1994. Available at: http://www.citadel.net/Risha/incest.html.

Reilly, T. P., et al. "Children's Conceptions of Death and Personal Mortality." *Journal of Pediatric Psychology* 8 (1983).

Roeder, K. A. "A Comparison of Adolescent Psychiatric Patients and Their Siblings with Regard to Ego Development and Self-Esteem." Doctoral dissertation, University of Hartford, 1990.

Rosen, H. "When a Sibling Dies." *International Journal of Family Psychiatry* 7 (1986).

Russell, D. E. H. *The Secret Trauma: Incest in the Lives of Girls and Women.* New York: Basic Books, 1986.

Schaefer, C. E., and H. C. Millman. *How to Help Children with Common Problems.* Northvale, N.J.: Jason Aronson, 1994.

Seligman, M. "Sources of Psychological Disturbance Among Siblings of Handicapped Children." *Personnel and Guidance Journal* 61 (1983).

Staples, B. "Special Education Is Not a Scandal." *New York Times Magazine,* 21 (September 1997): 64–65.

Straus, M. A., R. J. Gelles, and S. K. Steinmetz. *Behind Closed Doors: Violence in the American Family.* New York: Anchor, 1980.

Vanderbilt, H. "Incest: A Chilling Report." *Lears,* February, 1992, 51.

APPENDIX

FURTHER READING

American Psychiatric Association. *Diagnostic and Statistical Manual of Mental Disorders.* 4th ed. Washington, D.C.: American Psychiatric Press, 1994.

————. *Textbook of Psychiatry.* 2d ed. Washington, D.C.: American Psychiatric Press, 1994.

————. *Treatment of Psychiatric Disorders.* 2d ed. 2 vols. Washington, D.C.: American Psychiatric Press, 1995.

Bank, S., and M. Kahn. *The Sibling Bond.* New York: Basic Books, 1982.

Bass, E., and L. Davis. *The Courage to Heal: A Guide for Women Survivors of Child Sexual Abuse.* 3d ed. HarperCollins, 1994.

Grollman, E. A. *Straight Talk About Death for Teenagers: How to Cope with Losing Someone You Love.* Boston: Beacon Press, 1993.

Marsh, D. T., R. M. Dickens, and E. F. Torrey. *How to Cope with Mental Illness in Your Family: A Self-Care Guide for Siblings, Offspring, and Parents.* New York: Putnam, 1998.

Meyer, D., and P. Vadasy. *Living with a Brother or Sister with Special Needs: A Book for Sibs.* 2d ed. Seattle: University of Washington Press, 1996. Available at: http://www.chmc.org/departmt/sibsupp/.

National Center for Victims of Crime. "Infolink: Incest." 1997. Available at: http://www.nvc.org/infolink/info29.html/.

Overbeck, B., and J. Overbeck. *Helping Children Cope with Loss.* Dallas, TX: TLC Group, 1995.

Wiehe, V. *Sibling Abuse.* Toronto: Lexington Books, 1990.

Woolis, R., and A. Hatfied. *When Someone You Love Has a Mental Illness: A Handbook for Family, Friends, and Caregivers.* New York: Jeremy P. Tarcher, 1992.

APPENDIX

GLOSSARY

Americans with Disabilities Act: a federal statute, enacted in 1990, that forbids discrimination against physically and mentally disabled persons. It covers employers and such providers of public services as schools, hospitals, and mass-transit agencies.

Anxiety: a psychological condition in which an individual experiences tension or vague dread despite the absence of any specific threat. Its physical symptoms may include (among others) tense muscles, quickened heartbeat and breathing, and profuse sweating. Like depression and guilt, the condition may result from unresolved psychic conflicts, including those involving siblings.

Depression: a psychological condition in which an individual experiences generalized, persistent, and intense sadness without any specific external cause. Among its many physical and psychological symptoms are fatigue and diminished energy, changes in sleeping and eating patterns, loss of pleasure in the ordinary activities of life, feelings of hopelessness, and thoughts of suicide. Like anxiety and guilt, the condition may result from unresolved psychic conflicts, including those involving siblings.

Down syndrome (DS): a physical disorder resulting from the presence of an extra, third chromosome in an individual's genetic makeup. Characteristics often found in persons with DS include floppy muscles, slanted eyes, a flat-bridged nose, and some level of mental retardation. The disorder is also known as Down's syndrome and mongolism.

Group therapy: a form of psychological treatment grounded in the belief that many of a person's difficulties spring from, and can be resolved by, interacting with and adapting to others. Ideally, the therapeutic group reflects the outside world. Although sessions may be directed by a therapist, the heart of the approach lies in bringing members themselves to understand that other individuals suffer from similar problems, permitting them to experiment with new ways of interacting in the safety of the group, and allowing them to continue the treatment while they try out their new approaches in the larger society. Alcoholics Anonymous, a "peer group" directed and controlled entirely by its members, is the best-known example of this approach.

Guilt: commonly, an ethically based sense of remorse for some misdeed. As used in this book, an emotionally based feeling that one could or should have acted differently in a situation that was, in essence, beyond one's control (such as the death of a sister or brother). Guilt as an emotion can often become nearly overwhelming, beyond all relation to the person's actual past behavior. In this form such feelings can feed both anxiety and depression, intensifying and prolonging their various physical and psychological symptoms.

Incest avoidance: a hypothesis proposed early in the twentieth century by the Finnish anthropologist Edward Westermarck. Briefly, it holds that the tight bonds developed by living in close proximity during early childhood cause the persons involved to become innately averse to sexual relations with each other. This is contrary to Sigmund Freud's view that humans are incestuous by nature and are restrained from having sex with family members only by cultural and social pressures. Later research with animals has tended to support Westermarck's position.

Individual therapy: a form of psychological treatment grounded in the belief that many of a person's difficulties lie within the self. This approach assumes that problems can best be resolved by becoming aware of their origins, interpreting them in this light, and then confronting them, all under the guidance of a personal psychotherapist. The therapeutic systems developed by Sigmund Freud, Carl G. Jung, and Alfred Adler are among the best-known examples of this method of treatment.

Individuals with Disabilities Education Act (IDEA): the successor statute to the federal Education for All Handicapped Children Act of 1975. Among its guarantees for physically or mentally disabled children are free public schooling, an "individualized education program" for each pupil, and instruction carried on whenever possible with nondisabled, "mainstream" peers.

Parental incest: sexual contact, with or without intercourse, between natural parents and children or between those acting as parents and the girls and boys in their care. Its most frequently reported form involves abuse of daughters by their fathers. Besides possibly involving physical injury, such behavior almost always leads to significant emotional and psychological problems.

Pervasive developmental disorder (PDD): a physical ailment that manifests itself in children over time. It leaves them more demanding and less able to adapt to change as they age, and in some cases renders them unable to understand or display particular emotions.

Psychic trauma: as described by Sigmund Freud and others, an emotionally wounding childhood incident (such as an act of incest) that evolves into a psychological disturbance in adulthood. Treatment involves recalling and confronting the event under the guidance of a psychotherapist.

Sibling: commonly, a full brother or sister. As used in this book, any girl or boy who has grown up in one's household—a stepbrother, a half sister, an adopted child, a foster child, and so on.

Sibling aggression: conflict between brothers and sisters that expands beyond normal rivalry or rough play by mutual consent. In some cases, serious injury inflicted by beating or the use of a weapon, or even deliberate killing, may be involved.

Sibling incest: sexual contact, with or without intercourse, between brothers and sisters. Such relationships should not be confused with the sexual curiosity and explorations of young children of about the same age, which are a normal part of maturation. Although the acts may be either heterosexual or homosexual, the most frequently reported form of incest between siblings involves the abuse of younger girls by older boys. Whether the behavior is ongoing or has ended, professional counseling for all the persons involved is desirable.

Sibling rivalry: continuing discord between brothers and sisters; it may range from arguments between preschoolers over a toy to competition between adolescents over social status. So long as the conflict does not show signs of becoming deep, enduring, and angry (and thus perhaps leading to sibling aggression), it should be treated as an inevitable and generally positive part of growing up.

Support group: a set of persons who come together to discuss mutual psychological and emotional problems. Formally organized, such gatherings generally include a psychotherapist, who frequently plays a directing role.

Support system: an informal, leaderless body of persons to whom an individual may turn for counsel. Usually, relatives, friends, associates, members of the clergy, and the like may be involved, either individually or collectively.

APPENDIX

INDEX

APPENDIX

PICTURE CREDITS

Senior Consulting Editor Carol C. Nadelson, M.D., is president and chief executive officer of the American Psychiatric Press, Inc., staff physician at Cambridge Hospital, and Clinical Professor of Psychiatry at Harvard Medical School. In addition to her work with the American Psychiatric Association, which she served as vice president in 1981–83 and president in 1985–86, Dr. Nadelson has been actively involved in other major psychiatric organizations, including the Group for the Advancement of Psychiatry, the American College of Psychiatrists, the Association for Academic Psychiatry, the American Association of Directors of Psychiatric Residency Training Programs, the American Psychosomatic Society, and the American College of Mental Health Administrators. In addition, she has been a consultant to the Psychiatric Education Branch of the National Institute of Mental Health and has served on the editorial boards of several journals. Doctor Nadelson has received many awards, including the Gold Medal Award for significant and ongoing contributions in the field of psychiatry, the Elizabeth Blackwell Award for contributions to the causes of women in medicine, and the Distinguished Service Award from the American College of Psychiatrists for outstanding achievements and leadership in the field of psychiatry.

Consulting Editor Claire E. Reinburg, M.A., is editorial director of the American Psychiatric Press, Inc., which publishes about 60 new books and six journals a year. She is a graduate of Georgetown University in Washington, D.C., where she earned bachelor of arts and master of arts degrees in English. She is a member of the Council of Biology Editors, the Women's National Book Association, the Society for Scholarly Publishing, and Washington Book Publishers.

As director of Write Stuff Editorial Service in New York City, **Elizabeth Russell Connelly** has written and edited for medical and business journals, trade magazines, high-tech firms, and various book publishers. She earned an MBA from New York University's Stern School in 1993 and a certificate in language studies from Freiburg Universitaet (Switzerland) in 1985. Her published work includes a global studies book for young adults; more than 14 Access travel guides covering North America, the Caribbean, and Europe; and several volumes in Chelsea House Publishers' ENCYCLOPEDIA OF PSYCHOLOGICAL DISORDERS.